Green Giants

Rainforests of the Pacific Northwest

By Tom Parkin

earth
care
books

Douglas & McIntyre
Toronto/Vancouver

Douglas & McIntyre Ltd.
585 Bloor Street West
Toronto, Ontario M6G 1K5

Canadian Cataloguing in Publication Data

Parkin, Tom, 1951–
    Green giants : rainforests of the Pacific Northwest

(Earthcare books)
Includes index.
ISBN 1-55054-201-X

1. Rain forest ecology — Northwest Coast of North
America. 2. Rain forests — Northwest Coast of North
America. 3. Forest ecology — Northwest, Pacific.
I. Title. II. Series.

QH104.5.P32P37 1992 508.315′2′09795 C92-093155-3

All photographs by Tom Parkin except p. 6, MaryAnn
Parkin; p. 16, p. 29 top right, D. Horwood; p. 24,
p. 31 top, Mark Hobson; p. 28 top, Mark Nyhof; p. 30
top, Wayne Campbell; p. 30 bottom, Ervio Sian.

Several authorities have scanned sections of the text.
They include Ken Drushka, co-author of *Three Men
and a Forester*; Allison Nicholson, research ecologist,
B.C. Ministry of Forests; Robert A. Cannings, Chief of
Biology, Royal British Columbia Museum; Dr. Denis P.
Lavender, Department of Forest Sciences, University of
British Columbia; J. Charles Scrivener, research
biologist at the federal government's Pacific Biological
Station. All opinions expressed, however, are those of
the author.

Designed by Michael Solomon
Printed and bound in Hong Kong

Contents

INTRODUCTION

All around the world, people are talking about tropical rainforests. Many countries are cutting down their forests for wood, to make room for industry, and for farmland. Our whole planet is being affected. Plants and animals are becoming extinct, our climate is changing, and the lives of people who live in those forests often are not improved.

Because I wanted to see such forests for myself, I went to Australia and to Costa Rica in Central America to explore their wonders. There I saw and photographed peculiar creatures, beautiful flowers, and fascinating trees. I learned all I could, and became excited about writing a book about those foreign forests.

But when I came home, people were talking about the northern rainforests — the ones that lie

Coastal Temperate Rainforests of the World ●

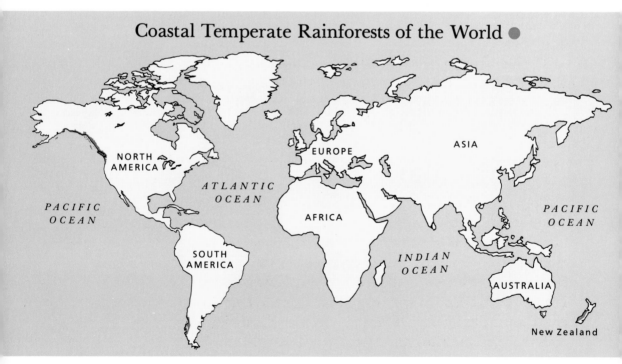

NORTH AMERICA

ATLANTIC OCEAN

PACIFIC OCEAN

EUROPE

ASIA

AFRICA

PACIFIC OCEAN

SOUTH AMERICA

INDIAN OCEAN

AUSTRALIA

New Zealand

along the west coast of Canada and the United States. They still are. They say trees are being logged too fast. Too little land is being saved for parks, and the environment is suffering. Forest loss isn't just a problem in tropical countries. Only recently have people in Canada and the United States recognized how little we value and understand rainforests in our own backyards.

Coastal forests in North America's Pacific Northwest are too far from the equator to be tropical, but they're still called rainforests. On the ocean-facing slopes of Alaska, British Columbia, Washington, and Oregon you'll find forests as special, as complex, and as valuable as those in the tropics. These forests, too, are threatened by extensive logging.

So I wrote a different book — this one — to help you discover temperate rainforests for yourself. Most often this book describes the forest I know best — the rainforest of Canada — but many of the problems we face in B.C. are common in the United States as well. I hope you'll become as concerned about these northern rainforests as I am. Your opinion will make a difference to the future.

CHAPTER 1
Shrinking Land of Giants

Most people think of tropical places when they hear the word rainforest. Tropical rainforests are jungles in countries close to the equator. Their temperatures are warm and their air is humid year round. But rainforests also grow in other regions of the world, including cool countries. These are called temperate rainforests.

Tropical and temperate rainforests aren't really similar. They have different plants, different creatures, and different environments. Temperate forests have fewer species of plants and animals than tropical rainforests, but more individuals of each kind. Still, both forest types grow gigantic evergreen trees and receive more rain than most places on earth.

In tropical rainforests, the rain usually falls evenly throughout the year. In temperate rainforests, there tends to be one long wet season with a short dry summer. During the summer on the northwest coast of North America, fog often provides the moisture that plants need. Temperatures are mild all year.

The Pacific Northwest is the most densely forested region of North America. The type of temperate rainforest growing here isn't found anywhere else in the world. Here stand hemlock, cedar, spruce, and

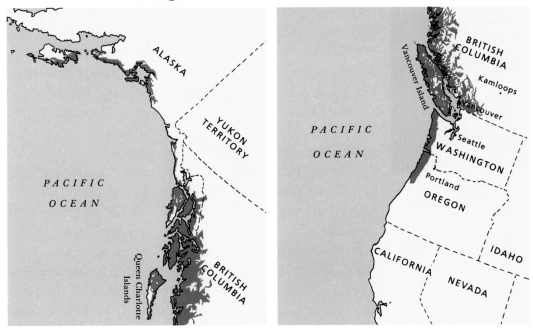

fir — evergreen conifers (cone-bearing trees with needle-like leaves). Clouds blowing from the Pacific Ocean drop rain on the west side of a mountain chain before passing over to the drier interior. Rainfall is 2.5 to 4 meters (8 to 13 feet) each year. That's well over your height!

In this climate, evergreens can grow tall very quickly. Other places in North America are wet or grow big trees, too, but none contain true rainforest.

In Canada, rainforest grows only along the coast of the province of British Columbia. This small strip contains close to half of this country's useful timber, including all the largest and oldest trees. Some of these forests support more living material than the densest tropical jungles. That's because temperate conifers tend to be taller and have wider trunks than tropical trees. Our tallest rise 95 meters (312 feet) in height — as high as a 30-storey building! Some are more than 1,000 years old.

Being alone under such remarkable trees can be both humbling and inspiring. They soar so high you feel like an ant beneath them. It's not unlike stepping into a cathedral. The feeling is magical and peaceful. For some people, forests are like outdoor temples. Visitors enter them with respect and admiration. They come away knowing these places are special in their lives, and precious to this planet.

Unfortunately, virgin temperate rainforests are becoming scarce. For more than 100 years, Pacific Northwest rainforests have been cut for lumber and to make room for farmland, cities, and roads. Only a small amount has been saved as parks. Outside of parks where they are protected, comparatively few forests are left that haven't been disturbed. In fact, at current cutting rates, virtually all of B.C.'s commercial rainforest will be gone in less than 30 years.

Our temperate rainforests are disappearing because vast areas are being logged by clear-cutting. Clear-cuts are areas from which all the forest has been removed by men and machines. They upset people because they look like a mess left after a huge explosion. Even loggers agree clear-cuts are ugly until young trees "green them up."

After a forest has been clear-cut, the ground is covered with splintered wood, stumps, dust, and litter thrown away by loggers. Hardly a living plant shows. Often the whole mess (called slash) is burned to help young trees get started on bare soil. The stumps and left-behind wood turn black.

Clear-cutting is used throughout much of the world, and it is the most popular logging method in North America. That's because it's the simplest, safest, and cheapest way to log and grow new forests. Clear-cut areas are easy to look after and aren't a hazard to workers (such as from falling trees and

GREEN GIANTS

Many kinds of trees grow in our magnificent rainforests, but the four most important timber species are western hemlock, western redcedar, Douglas-fir, and Sitka spruce. Except for the redwoods of California, these are the tallest trees in the world.

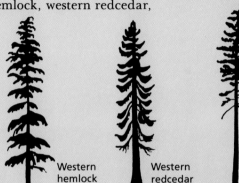
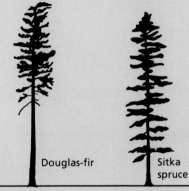

Western hemlock   Western redcedar   Douglas-fir   Sitka spruce

Western hemlock

Canada's biggest hemlock is in Pacific Rim National Park on the west coast of Vancouver Island, British Columbia. It stands 55 meters (180 feet) tall, with a trunk circumference of 8 meters (26 feet). It would take you and nine friends to encircle it with your arms. A fatter but shorter hemlock grows in Quinault River Valley, Olympic National Park, Washington.

Western redcedar

In 1990 the world's largest cedar was discovered in Vancouver Island's Pacific Rim National Park. It stands 20 storeys (59 meters or 194 feet) tall and 6 meters (20 feet) through. This tree may be around 2,000 years old, which means it could have sprouted while Jesus Christ was alive.

Douglas-fir

The largest Douglas-fir now living is in California. But a monster cut in 1895 in North Vancouver, B.C., was even taller. That one measured 127 meters (417 feet) from bottom to top and 7.5 meters (25 feet) through at the base. Its bark alone was 40 centimeters (16 inches) thick. That's thicker than the walls of your home.

The highest "Doug fir" now growing in B.C. is on the west coast of Vancouver Island near Port Renfrew. This one is 74 meters (243 feet) high and 12 meters (40 feet) around the base.

Sitka spruce

The world's largest Sitka spruce was found in 1988 in Carmanah Valley on the west coast of Vancouver Island. The "Carmanah Giant" is 95 meters (312 feet) tall and more than 3 meters (10 feet) thick at the base. Most Sitkas grow to an average of 60 meters (197 feet) in height and 2 meters (6 feet) in diameter.

IDENTIFY THE TREES

A tall tree can be hard to identify because its leaves are so high. Instead, look at its bark or shape. Study cones and branches that have fallen beneath.

Western hemlock
This tree has graceful branches and a bent-over top. Its cones are less than 2 centimeters (3/4 inch) long, but one tree can produce over half a million seeds each year. Hemlock seedlings can survive deep shade on the forest floor.

Douglas-fir
Large Douglas-firs have very thick furrowed bark. Their cones have three protruding forks under each scale. Young Douglas-firs have smooth bark with little blisters of pitch that smell wonderful when you pop them.

Western redcedar
This tree has thin stringy bark, cinnamon to gray in color. The wood smells a bit like pineapple. The dark-green leaves form flat, fern-like fronds. Old trees are buttressed and broad at the base. This gives the tree better support.

Sitka spruce
This coastal spruce has big loose scales of bark. The cones are 8 to 10 centimeters (3 to 4 inches) long with wrinkled edges.

limbs). Because clear-cutting is less laborious than other logging methods, people don't have to pay as much for wood and paper products made from trees cut this way.

Clear-cutting is also an advantage because it removes diseased trees. If only some trees were cut from an area, diseased trees might be left to infect nearby trees or those that grow afterwards. As well, trees such as Douglas-firs grow best in sunlight, so they will grow faster in a clear-cut than within existing forest.

The best method of clear-cutting is to scatter the cut sections, called "blocks," over a wide area. As these areas re-grow, a forest of different ages and species is created. This is better than scalping a whole valley or mountain, which is ecologically disastrous.

Clear-cutting is a problem throughout the Northwest. In British Columbia, however, so many areas are being clear-cut that less and less virgin rainforest

Clearcut at the edge of Carmanah Valley. Due to public pressure, half of Carmanah Valley has been preserved as a provincial park to save big trees.

is left between the blocks. Not only is there an increasing number of clear-cuts, but the areas are huge. A typical B.C. clear-cut is ten times the size of a clearcut in the coniferous forests of Sweden. After a while, cut-blocks start to join together, forming enormous open areas. Some cover entire mountainsides.

We know clear-cuts make life difficult for fish and wildlife. They can be harmful to soil and to streams. They even change the climate because they have no trees to catch and hold the rain and fog. Their soil becomes dry. Winds sweep through the surrounding

Clearcut on Vancouver Island. The Sierra Club has warned that this region is in danger of losing all of its ancient forests within ten years.

trees more forcefully, sometimes blowing them down.

Problems also develop when clear-cuts are burned after logging to remove slash. Other problems are caused when fertilizers are used to help seedlings grow faster, or when chemicals are sprayed over the trees to kill insects and plants that harm them.

However, the biggest problem is that huge areas of temperate rainforest are simply being destroyed by logging. For example, in Oregon, less than one-tenth of the original forests remain. They've been so heavily cut that some creatures that depend on them are also disappearing.

North Americans have always thought that rainforests were only threatened in poorer countries, and that our own resources were well managed. We became concerned by the consequences to the world's climate, the extinction of species, and the rights of native peoples. Many schools and groups raised money to purchase land for parks in Central and South America. Some of us have traveled to visit countries such as Belize and Brazil to appreciate the wonder and beauty of their tropical rainforests before they disappear.

Now the same thing is happening at home. People from all over the world are coming to see the magnificence of our temperate rainforests. They tell us there are no forests like them on earth, and that we should preserve them. Scientists studying our rainforests are discovering new things about them all the time.

We find it hard to admit this is happening to us. We know that changing the situation will be difficult. But slowly we're beginning to appreciate what we hear. More and more people now want to understand why our temperate rainforests are so special, and why they are worth saving.

CHAPTER 2

Tall Trees and Large Logs

Walking through a temperate rainforest can be confusing. There are too many plants, shades of green, and places to look. Pacific Northwest rainforests started growing after the Ice Age ended about 12,000 years ago, so they've had plenty of time to develop a complex habitat. If you don't take time to look closely, you might pass through without noticing much at all. But by concentrating on one thing at a time, and by being quiet and curious, you begin to notice things.

First you may notice all kinds of ferns and mosses. They love cool, moist places near the forest floor. You notice how thickly plants grow. Many keep their leaves year-round, and they grow on top of one another. Some are simply climbing high toward the limited sunlight; others are helping decompose trees that have died and fallen. The decomposers are mostly mushrooms and other fungi. Mushrooms grow especially well after the first rains of autumn, springing up in colors of beige, red, and orange.

And if you really concentrate and keep quiet, after a while small birds and maybe a deer will begin to move through the undergrowth.

Each rainforest grove looks different. Each has different sizes and species of trees. Some have thick shrubbery growing under the trees; other groves have open mossy floors. But in each case, if these four things are visible, you're in an ancient Pacific northwest rainforest:

1. Large conifers with a multi-layered canopy
2. Large standing snags
3. Nurse logs
4. Large logs lying in streams

Sap carries nutrients and water up and down a tree's trunk. The tree protects this food pathway with its skin of bark. Even so, insects and fungi sometimes break through to reach what lies beneath. The bark of this Sitka spruce flakes off as the tree grows and expands. New bark grows on the inside; the oldest bark is on the outside.

1. Large conifers with a multi-layered canopy

It takes a long time for a rainforest to mature — it isn't just a young forest grown old or tall. Trees have to be at least 175 to 250 years old before the complex community of a northwest rainforest begins to form around them.

Most virgin rainforests are much older than the individual trees within them. Several generations of trees may have lived previously in an ancient forest — meaning trees may have grown in such a place for thousands of years. Such communities have many different sizes, ages, and species of plants and animals.

A mature forest has at least three layers: tall trees, younger trees, and undergrowth. Can you pick out plants in each of these layers?

Each species in a rainforest is there for a reason, though we don't yet know what each contributes to the benefit of other organisms. And if we don't know how something works, we can't re-create it ourselves. This means that while foresters have learned how to plant trees, a rainforest has yet to be grown by people.

The canopy — the umbrella of branches overhead — forms two layers. The top layer is made by the big trees, whose branches may be carrying a hanging garden of small plants including lichens, mosses, and sometimes ferns. These small plants don't need soil in which to root.

Lower down are immature trees waiting for a chance to replace their parents. When a giant falls, the sun shines through the hole in the top layer, and younger trees put on a growth spurt to fill the space.

A third layer may be formed by shrubs like salal, devil's club, red huckleberry, and salmonberry. Bears and birds like to eat the fruit of these last two. Together, these low plants are called undergrowth (see Chapter 3).

An ancient rainforest is a complicated environment. Even when clear-cut commercial forests are replanted, true rainforest never returns. Though the next crop (called "second-growth") grows to cover the scar, logging companies intend to cut it down 80, 100, or 120 years later. That's enough time for trees to grow large enough for lumber, but not enough time to develop a new rainforest community. Unlike virgin forests, the trees in a planted forest are the same age and much the same size. Such a forest is green and can grow well, but it's not the mixed community of nature.

2. Large standing snags

Snags are dead trees from which most of the limbs have fallen. In some areas of the United States, snags are left standing, but in British Columbia, a law says loggers must cut them down for reasons of safety when they are working nearby. But snags are valuable. People use them for firewood. Numerous insects, birds, and mammals use them as supermarkets, for food storage, and as a place to raise their young.

Insects burrow in the rotting wood because it's easy eating compared to the hard wood of live trees. Birds such as Chestnut-backed Chickadees and Red-breasted Nuthatches probe the loose bark looking for insect treats. During cold months when food is scarce or covered by snow, such energy-giving insects are vital for bird survival.

Snags usually have old nest holes left by woodpeckers. Birds such as owls and Brown Creepers use the holes for spring nesting sites as well, but such cavities are especially important in winter. Since winter nights are long and wet, birds sleep in these holes, sometimes sharing with roostmates of a different species. This keeps them all warm, dry, and safe.

Second-growth forests don't provide the snags essential to winter survival because their dead trees aren't thick enough to make good nests or winter

Snags can be dangerous because limbs or broken tops can fall on people below.

shelters. And in second-growth, there are few original snags left because most have been cut. As a result, second-growth forests have fewer birds. This has become such a problem in Germany that foresters have put up nestboxes as places for birds to raise their young and find shelter.

3. Nurse logs

Rainforests are great recyclers. When a tree dies and falls, it takes centuries to decompose, gradually turning into a natural compost that fertilizes the soil. In one hectare (2 1/2 acres) of ancient rainforest, there can be nearly 300 trees decaying on the floor.

These rotten logs nourish countless insects, animals, fungi, and plants — even microscopic bacteria. Such creatures help break down the log into soil. In doing so, they also find life for themselves in the log. In fact, there is twice as much living material in a "dead" log as there is in a living tree! That's because healthy trees are solid and don't have creatures or fungi living within them.

Seeds of other trees, especially western hemlock, sprout on the surface of these fallen logs. They send roots through the rotting wood to absorb nutrients, moisture, and warmth. Because these fallen trees help such young sprouts, they're called nurse logs.

When trees grow on nurse logs, after a century or so, the log breaks down completely, exposing the roots growing through them. This can make trees look as if they're balancing on one-handed pushups. If the nurse log was a big one, several trees probably grew on it. Sometimes you find as many as ten trees standing in a row. Their nurse log may be long gone, but you know how they got that way. This feature is called a colonnade.

Nurse logs are found infrequently in planted for-

This suspended nurse log nurtures a series of young hemlocks. They have grown in a poor place because they may die when the log eventually breaks and collapses under their weight.

A colonnade.

ests. Like snags, they disappear because commercial forests are cut too soon for trees to die and rot and nourish a younger generation of trees. Over a long time, forests could grow more poorly because they're not allowed to recycle their organic material into soil. This is happening in the managed forests of Germany, for instance.

4. Large logs lying in streams

Even when they fall into creeks, dead trees give life to other organisms. Large trunks act like dams, and gravel fills in behind them. A small waterfall and pool form below or under the log. Water flows around other logs, creating eddies.

A creek with such backwaters and fallen wood has more life in it and on its banks than one that flows fast and straight. That's because insects that live in water or eat tree leaves can survive without being swept away. Those insects and the woody cover attract animals such as fish and salamanders, which in turn attract other creatures.

Logs in the water rot very slowly, and can remain in a stream for over one hundred years. Fallen trees that collect in streams help prevent streambank erosion during high water. Those that stand above the water keep it shaded and cool. Such clear, cold water is ideal for salmon and trout, and the Pacific Northwest is famous for its fishing.

The temperate rainforests aren't special just because they grow huge trees that are becoming scarce. They're also special because they're ancient and

Logs lying in coastal streams help slow the rush of water. This prevents erosion, and provides places for fish to hide and feed, as well as bridges for hikers!

diverse. They're not wood factories for lumber and pulp mills, but forests able to re-create themselves without us. They provide habitat for fish and wildlife and places for recreation and nature study. Their clear streams provide drinking water for our cities.

When we clear-cut the big trees, knock down all the snags, haul away the timber, burn the downed logs, and then spray herbicides on the recovering undergrowth, we halt the natural development of a rainforest. Hundreds of years were necessary to develop it, and maybe a thousand years to form the soils on which those forests first grew. With our current forestry methods, we may well eliminate the possibility that temperate rainforests as we know them will ever grow back.

Until recently, many people thought of big trees simply as big profits. When they saw trees that had grown old and begun to rot, they considered them worthless. Now we know that everything in a forest has value to other organisms and contributes to the ongoing survival of the forest as a whole. Now we know enough to ask questions about the way forest companies and governments manage our rainforests.

CHAPTER 3
The Forest Floor

If you watch adventure movies, you may have seen people swinging machetes to cut their way through jungle undergrowth. Undergrowth is the community of plants that grow near the forest floor, and each plant can be as tiny as a toadstool or the size of a sapling. In temperate rainforests, undergrowth can be as dense and difficult to walk through as any tropical jungle.

Despite being numerous, undergrowth plants have a hard life. Imagine yourself as a small flower under a canopy of big trees. There are advantages to living with such neighbors. They keep snow from burying you, the sun from drying you, and they protect you from windstorms.

But they also drop dead branches that might crush you. They take most of the essential minerals, water, and sunlight you need for life. That's because they have wider root systems, catch rain in their needles before it drops to the forest floor, and filter light with their canopy. In short, your neighbors change the climate beneath them.

Each plant has a way of overcoming the difficult climate on the forest floor. Some have eliminated their need for light. Others are able to steal nourishment from their neighbors. Still others have given up roots so they can live above the ground.

Plants that don't need light aren't green and don't have leaves — or at least have leaves too small to gather sunlight. For example, pink coralroot can grow in the darkest places of a forest. It absorbs all its energy from decaying matter in the soil.

Another group of plants doesn't need light, either. These plants grow *inside* trees. Called bracket fungi,

The bush called salal forms some of the thickest thickets in temperate rainforest. Its white bell-shaped flowers are followed by edible black berries. Natives once collected them for food. Today, twigs of salal are collected for the fresh-flower business, as a background for cut bouquets. Some coastal people make a living picking and selling such greenery.

An old Douglas-fir can have 66 million needles. They catch nearly all the sunshine before it reaches the forest floor. Small plants that survive in the undergrowth have different ways of overcoming such shade. Some, like this skunk cabbage, grow large leaves to gather the weak light. Other plants have leaves of a deep green color. This shows they have more food-making chemicals concentrated in their leaves.

they solve both the food and falling branch problems by feeding on dead or living wood. Normally they can't be seen, but when they mature, they produce a woody sort of fruit. This fruiting body looks like a shelf or bracket stuck on the tree trunk. Such fungi release fine dust-like spores into the air, which is how they reproduce.

Brackets are hard and last for years. Though slow-growing, bracket fungi eventually kill their host tree because they steal its energy and break the strength of its wood.

Other plants grow on trees without harming them. Such specialists are lichens, which cling to branches to find extra light. There are many kinds, but one lichen that some people recognize easily is old-man's beard. It's black and dangles from branches like whiskers.

Other lichens look like leaves without stems or roots. In fact, that's what lichens are. Lacking roots, they live on air and ingredients drawn from dust and rainwater that wash over them. Scientists have found more than 100 kinds of lichen in Pacific Northwest rainforests.

As lichens dangle from the limbs of trees, plants such as mosses gather along the upper part of the branches. Dust and dead needles fall into these pads, and soon a layer of vegetation begins to grow in this soil above the ground. The accumulation can be so great that a large tree may hold up a tonne (2,240 pounds) of "sky garden."

Eventually, a heavy limb weakens and plummets to the ground with all its load. These fallen limbs provide important winter food for deer and elk when snow covers other undergrowth plants. But even if a limb doesn't break off, there's a steady fall of organic material from such branches. Dead needles, bits of

lichen, and broken twigs are always tumbling down. They add nutrients to the soil as they decompose. The forest is perfectly organized to look after the survival of all its members.

Hundreds of species of ferns and mosses are also at home in the damp, dark conditions of Pacific Northwest rainforests. Moss grows so deep it can become a soft mattress on the forest floor. You can even sleep on a bed of moss!

There are so many plants living in the undergrowth that it can take years to learn them all. It's not important to remember every one, but many visitors overlook the undergrowth because they come to see trees. No forest grows without plants beneath it. A forest is a community. Each plant is there for a purpose, and each has an effect on other plants, on wildlife, and on people.

Left: Bracket fungus (sometimes called a conch) is a member of the mushroom family. This fruiting structure drops spores from its pale underside in order to reproduce.

Right: Lungwort lichen can look dead and dried out, but becomes green and soft as soon as it rains. It grows on the upper limbs of tall conifers.

Living wood has chemical defenses against attack by fungi. When a tree dies, the chemicals gradually break down and are no longer effective. Western redcedar contains a particularly potent chemical that helps the wood resist rot decades after it has been cut into lumber or falls in the forest. This enables cedar carvings like this Bella Coola mortuary figure to last more than one hundred years.

CHAPTER 4
Bears and Banana Slugs

British Columbia has more kinds of wildlife than any other province in Canada. As well, more animal species live *only* in B.C. than anywhere in the country. Not all these creatures live in the rainforest, but these facts show B.C. is important as the home of insects, amphibians, birds, and mammals — creatures that depend on one another and on a pure environment.

For example, B.C. is home to one-quarter of the world's grizzly bears. Grizzly bears require large areas of wilderness to survive. At one time these magnificent animals roamed over all the Pacific Northwest. Now their populations are seriously reduced — so much so that in 1991 these bears were placed on the Canadian endangered species list. Human settlement, mining, and logging have disturbed so much of this bear's former territory that there are few sanctuaries left. One of the last places grizzlies find safety is in coastal rainforest, where some of the largest bears in the world live.

Two and a half centuries ago, hundreds of thousands of grizzly bears lived from the Arctic to Mexico, and from the west coast to the center of the continent. Between 15,000 and 18,000 grizzlies now live in Canada's western provinces, but they have virtually disappeared from the lower 48 states of the U.S.

The blacktail deer of western forests move with changing snow conditions, and migrate up and down the coastal mountains.

As loggers build roads in the rainforest, grizzlies are losing important habitat. Fewer and fewer coastal valleys are left that haven't had some logging in them.

Other large animals are common in the temperate rainforest. Two examples are Roosevelt elk and black-tail deer. For decades, people assumed logging was good for deer and elk because these animals found plenty of food in clear-cuts during most of the year. But this assumption was wrong because no one went around to see what life was like for those animals during the most difficult season of the year.

Squirrels are very dependent on the seed crop of trees. If no seeds are produced, there are no squirrels. If the squirrel population declines, there will be fewer predators as well.

Most winters, the temperate climate of the northwest coast is easy to survive. But when the occasional one turns tough, deer and elk depend on the shelter provided by groves of very old trees. They find less wind among the big trunks, less snow because the canopy holds it off the ground, and more food exposed in the protected undergrowth. Even when snow covers the undergrowth, limbs breaking off above bring down lichens that these animals can feed on during a storm. When this virgin forest is logged, deer and elk find it harder to survive winters that are particularly severe.

A 5-centimeter (2-inch) millipede risks an exposed journey across the moss. Hundreds of such small creatures feed inside nurse logs and roam the forest floor. In turn, they provide food for amphibians, birds, and mammals.

This golden buprestid beetle eats tree needles and lays eggs in the bark of newly fallen trees. When the eggs hatch, the larvae burrow into the wood, starting the process of nurse log decomposition.

After clear-cut logging, it's impossible to return nature's balance quickly. Though the trees may be replanted, after 20 to 25 years the second-growth forest becomes too thick for survival of the undergrowth plants on which wildlife feed. And since most commercial forests will be cut and replaced every 80 to 100 years in the future, this perfectly balanced habitat will never return. This means wildlife populations that depend on virgin rainforest can never fully recover. Though the trees grow again, the community isn't the same; it isn't whole.

For example, remember the definition of temperate rainforest includes snags and large nurse logs, which can be nurseries for animals as well as for plants. Mammals such as pine martens make dens and raise their young in the cavities of snags or logs. Martens often hunt in trees, where they eat squirrels, their main food. If second-growth trees are too young to bear cones (which squirrels feed on), then the forest won't have martens, either. As well, since planted forests have few snags or nurse logs to serve as homes, martens rarely live there.

Nurse logs are wonderful places to look for forest wildlife. Some animals use them for homes; others use them simply as pathways above the tangled undergrowth. Bears will tear a log apart looking for mice and ant colonies to eat. Under the rotting bark, salamanders hunt for insects that help decompose the log. There are so many kinds of insects in a nurse log that scientists suspect they haven't discovered them all.

Of all animals found around logs, everybody recognizes the slug. Northwest rainforests have slippery, slow, slimy slugs. Big ones. These are banana slugs — which do grow as long as small bananas! These yellow and black slitherers are the largest snails without

Banana slugs have two pairs of tentacles on their heads. The longest tentacles have eyes at each tip, while the smaller ones help the slug to smell. A slug travels on a trail of slime secreted from a gland behind its mouth.

shells in the Pacific Northwest. They live to be four or five years old. What good are they? Well, banana slugs are terrific recyclers. They help decompose material on the forest floor. They eat almost any kind of leaf, lichen, fungus, or animal excrement. In turn, they are eaten by salamanders.

Only since the 1970s have scientists seriously studied our temperate rainforest ecology. There is such variety of wildlife here that biologists still don't know much about rainforest animals except for large species like deer and elk. Before anybody makes major decisions about how the land should be used, we need to know what's there. We also need to know how creatures, big and small, interact with their habitat, and what they need to survive.

Forests are the home of many creatures, and we can't forget their needs. We must not make the mistake of managing trees, but not forests. Though trees are a renewable resource, rainforests take centuries to renew themselves. Replacement forests will never be the same as the original. We must consider ancient trees, black-tailed deer, grizzlies, Bald Eagles, salmon, slugs, lichen, and mosses before we decide what to do with our rainforests.

Clear-cut logging and land development cause red-backed voles to disappear from certain areas. This may be because they depend on mushrooms that require tree roots to grow. When the trees disappear, so do the mushrooms and the voles.

CHAPTER 5

Wings in the Woods

Walking in the rainforest, you notice how quiet it is. No dry twigs snap underfoot; no leaves rustle. Wind may blow branches high above, and once in a while a leaning tree creaks against another, but few birds sing.

Not many birds live in temperate rainforest because there is less food for them than in other habitats. So birds that do live here are worth special notice.

The Pileated Woodpecker is the largest woodpecker living in North America.

You may hear the long, tinkling, trilling song of a tiny Winter Wren. This round-bodied wren has a tail that sticks straight up. It flits through dense undergrowth, catching spiders and small insects. Winter Wrens are hard to spot because their brown color hides them in the shade and amidst the brown wood. They have adapted to life near the dark forest floor.

In the distance, you might hear a sort of rapid rapping — *brrat-a-tat-tat*. If you look up the trunks of dead trees you may spot a big black-and-white bird with a red crest. It will be perched on the side of the snag, pounding its bill deep into the tree. The Pileated Woodpecker feeds on insects that live in dying and dead trees. This bird pries off loose bark and hammers large holes into wood, searching for a meal.

The favorite food of the Pileated Woodpecker is carpenter ants. These ants usually create colonies in large decaying trees. Sometimes these nests contain thousands of ants. Few trees die in young second-growth, and the ones that do are not thick enough for the ants to chew out a colony. Thus both carpenter ants and Pileated Woodpeckers live mostly in ancient rainforests.

Snags are year-round storehouses of high-quality bird food. There are usually six snags in half a hectare (about an acre) of Pacific Northwest rainforest.

Bald Eagle and nest.

The Steller's Jay finds its food on the ground, including fallen seeds of evergreen trees. Sometimes it buries the seeds for winter use. If it forgets these locations, the seeds sprout in the spring.

Another bird that needs mature forest to survive is the magnificent Bald Eagle. It's not really bald, but has a white head and tail feathers. One-quarter of all Bald Eagles in the world live in B.C. Most nest in tall trees close to the sea. They need big trees because their nests are big. They make them with sticks, adding more each year until the nest might weigh as much as a tonne (2,240 pounds).

When loggers cut close to the water's edge, they log trees that eagles might use for homes. If there aren't any good trees, the eagles have no place to build nests or raise chicks. Gradually their numbers will decline. Though loggers usually save trees that already have nests in them, these trees are often blown down later because they have no neighboring trees to protect them during high winds. In the United States, a law says nobody may cut any tree near an eagle perch or nest.

Other birds neither feed nor live in the rainforest, but still depend on them. This is true of Rhinoceros Auklets. Rhinoceros Auklets spend most of their lives on the Pacific Ocean. They swim, sleep, and eat at sea, well away from the mainland. Their food is fish.

Rhinoceros Auklets breed in coastal colonies between southeastern Alaska and northwestern Washington (although they used to live as far south as California). The youngster remains in the burrow until it can fly, so the parents must bring it fish from the sea.

Spotted Owl.

But each spring, these birds fly ashore to nest on remote coastal islands.

Auklets have difficulty walking on land, and they are unable to perch in trees. This makes them easy prey. To avoid trouble, they come ashore under the cover of darkness and dig deep burrows among the roots of large trees. This way they avoid being seen in daylight when they're so vulnerable, and they escape predators that would capture them if they nested above ground.

When rainforest on coastal islands is cut, we sometimes destroy the only place auklets can raise their young. Temperate rainforests are extremely important for survival of a bird that few people have ever seen.

For decades, biologists searched for nesting evidence of another small seabird called a Marbled Murrelet. They thought about 45,000 murrelets nested along B.C.'s coast, but never found any eggs or chicks. Biologists knew the birds were nesting because they saw them floating at sea during the day, then flying over the forest at dusk. But where the mysterious Marbled Murrelet laid its eggs was not discovered until the summer of 1990.

That year, biologists used mountaineering equipment to climb huge spruce trees on the west coast of Vancouver Island. The climbers strung ropes, hanging platforms and ladders up and down Sitka spruce that were more than 70 meters (230 feet) tall. It was North America's first, and the world's highest, treetop station. The researchers were so high they had to communicate with ground crews using two-way radios.

Twelve storeys off the ground, biologists found gnarled limbs so huge that other plants grew on them. The biggest branches had thick pads of moss on their upper side. On one was a depression with some feathers and shell fragments. It was a Marbled Murrelet nest! Evidently the chick had already "flown the coop," but biologists are confident they'll soon find an occupied nest.

We still don't know much about Marbled Murrelets. We do know one-tenth of the world population lives in B.C., and that the birds are on the threatened species list. This means they could become endangered without our help. One thing we can do is save their primary nesting habitat — old temperate rainforest.

Though Marbled Murrelets also live in the United States, British Columbia has more original rainforest left than the states of Washington, Oregon, and California combined. This means B.C. has an especially important role in keeping Marbled Murrelets from extinction.

Other birds depend on the temperate rainforest, and some of them are threatened, too. For example, in the U.S., laws now require areas of forest be saved for the secretive Spotted Owl. But a few reserves set aside aren't enough for some species if surrounding lands are barren of trees. The Spotted Owl will likely become extinct if logging continues, since they need large areas of virgin forest to survive. They feed mainly on flying squirrels and other ancient forest rodents, and each nesting pair needs 800 to 1,200 hectares (2,000 to 3,000 acres) just to raise their young.

Much talk has been made about the cost of preservation. Spotted Owls have been called "the Billion-Dollar Owl" by those unhappy about its protection. Like other wildlife, birds are but indicators of ecological trouble due to our huge devastation of their environment. They are not the problem — we are.

Marbled Murrelets breed on the coast between Alaska and central California. As many as 5,000 may nest in Washington State. The destruction of mature forest is a great threat to their continued survival, especially in California and Oregon.

Winter Wrens often nest in a cavity in the earthy roots of an upturned tree. This one is carrying food to its young.

CHAPTER 6

Salmon Stream

Most people don't think fish live in rainforests, but they do! Even though they swim in rivers and streams, fish need trees for survival. That's because trees shade their water, keeping it at temperatures freshwater fish prefer. Trees also prevent bank erosion and prevent sediment from entering the water, keeping it clear. Water gives fish oxygen, just as the air gives oxygen to us; fish need clean water to breathe. And when trees fall into the water, they provide food for insects and habitat for fish, particularly Pacific salmon.

The life cycle of the salmon is a wonder of nature. This fish spends the beginning and end of its life in fresh water, and at least half of it at sea. Young salmon hatch from eggs laid in stream gravel by an adult female. They may spend one, two, or three years in the stream or a downstream lake before swimming to the ocean, where they quickly gain size and weight. In a year or more, they become old enough to lay eggs.

Spawning, or egg-laying, happens during the summer and fall. Somehow, every salmon that hatches in a stream knows when to return home. Each fish swims across the north Pacific Ocean, finds the right river, and travels up it to the very same stream where it hatched. There it finds a mate, spawns, and dies. No salmon lives longer than seven years, and each spawns only once.

Since a salmon must spawn soon after reaching its home stream, and has only one chance to do this, its freshwater habitat is extremely important. It's no accident that the best coastal salmon habitat occurs in forested watersheds. Thousands of rainforest riv-

Sockeye salmon in spawning bed, Vancouver Island. When streams flow over fallen trees, deep pools are formed in the stream's gravel. These provide shelter and food for both young fish and migrating adults.

ers and streams in our coastal mountains are home to salmon runs.

These fish fed northwest natives for thousands of years, and they are now sold to people around the world. Anglers come from other countries to catch them for fun as well as for food.

Many species of wildlife also depend on these salmon. Grizzlies and black bears travel down from the mountains to feast. They wade right into flowing waters to chomp migrating salmon in their mouths, or to swat them onto the bank. Bald Eagles and gulls gather along the banks or in overhanging trees, waiting for a dying fish to wash up nearby. The smell of rotten flesh is strong enough to wrinkle your nose, but it doesn't stop school classes from coming

Sockeye salmon turn bright red and green when returning to spawn. They may travel huge distances and overcome many obstacles to reach the stream where they were born.

to see this event. They learn the forest is very important in maintaining all this activity. Our temperate rainforests protect some of the purest flows of water on the continent.

For example, when a tree falls into a stream, it helps break the rush of water and traps the streambed gravel. The logs make the water swirl into pools and back-eddies. Sometimes they jam together in a pile. These are places small fish can hide from predators and rest out of the current. These are also places where insects hide in the gravel, eating the soggy leaves that have sunk to the bottom. Some insects feed on the carcasses of spawned salmon. In turn, these insects become fish food.

During the winter, rainfall increases. Stream levels rise and the water flows faster. Again, dead trees lying in the stream slow the flood and protect young salmon from being washed away. These logs and branches also prevent the stream from eroding its banks and making the water muddy. Dirty water suffocates fish, and the mud can bury salmon eggs.

When a forest is logged, streams flowing through it are affected. Slash may wash into the water, forming barriers to migrating salmon. If fish can't travel upstream to spawn, or downstream to mature in the sea, their population dies. If trees lining a stream are cut, sunlight heats the unshaded water. Temperatures which were formerly just right can become too uncomfortable for fish to survive.

Often the undergrowth and roots of trees are so damaged by logging machinery that they no longer hold the soil in place. Heavy rains wash the dirt and road gravel into the streams. On steep slopes, the lack of trees can cause whole hillsides to become soft and slide down into the water. In Oregon's Willamette National Forest, half of the man-made erosion

An angler poses with his catch—a spring salmon weighing more than 13 kilograms (30 pounds).

comes from logged areas, the other half from logging roads. These kinds of scars take years and years for nature to heal, and the salmon may not come back in your lifetime.

This is a serious problem. The American Fisheries Society is very concerned about salmon and trout across the West Coast states of California, Oregon, and Washington. A total of 214 populations of fish are actually threatened or endangered — meaning they could become extinct in those waters if not protected. Though not all of this problem is due to logging, improved forestry methods and habitat restoration will certainly help those fish using rainforest streams. Declining salmon and trout populations are hurting our culture and our economy.

All salmon die after spawning. Their bodies become fertilizer.

Another problem is flooding. Forests can absorb twenty times more rain than bare soil because plants absorb water, carry it on their leaves, or drain it off underground through old root systems. When whole valleys are clear-cut, the rain or meltwater runs very fast overland to the rivers, which will then flood if they are unable to carry it all. Far downstream from the logged areas, houses, highways, and farm livestock can be washed under filthy water. Millions of dollars of damage can be done. This problem is becoming widespread throughout the Pacific Northwest.

Salmon streams of the Pacific Northwest were once the best in the world. Though poor logging methods are just one cause of their sad decline, it is still a problem we can resolve. Rainforest streams must be treated with more respect, not just for pure drinking water, but to save salmon as food for wildlife as well as people. We may think we no longer take food from the forest, but we forget about the fish among the trees.

CHAPTER 7

Forests Forever

The temperate rainforests of the Pacific Northwest are threatened by poor logging practice. Can we repair this damage? What can we do to correct the problems we have created?

Some people believe if we stopped logging, our rainforest problems would be solved. But have you thought what life would be like without wood? Just imagine if, right now, everything around you made from trees suddenly disappeared. You might find yourself standing on a slab of concrete. You wouldn't be able to sit down because all furniture with wood frames would have collapsed. The building around you might be gone — or at least be missing its walls. Everything made of paper would be gone, so there would be no toilet paper, no comics — even this book would be gone. Only things made of metal, plastic, rubber, stone, and cloth would remain. Life would become very difficult.

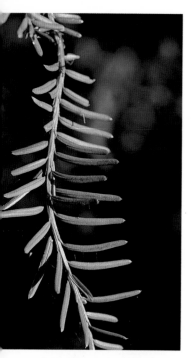

The western yew is found in coastal rainforests. Its bark and needles are being used to make a promising anti-cancer drug. As with tropical rainforests, there are likely other uses, yet to be discovered, for temperate rainforest plants.

The trees of the temperate rainforest are important to people in other parts of the world as well. Totem poles carved by today's native artists have been purchased by art-lovers around the world. Douglas-fir, first used to make masts for English sailing ships in the Pacific Northwest, is still used for shipbuilding today. Sitka spruce is perfect for piano and classical guitar parts. Cedar roof shingles are shipped throughout the world, and pulp and paper mills in the Pacific Northwest make paper for export to dozens of nations.

Each kind of tree is useful for special purposes because each has different properties. Sometimes there is no better substitute, so the wood is much in demand. Even people who don't live in the Pacific

Northwest create a demand for rainforest logging by their need for wood and paper products. If they knew and cared what happened as a result of their needs, would it be possible to do things differently?

Trees also have value just standing in a rainforest. For years, artists have found rainforests to be special places in which to paint, draw, carve, and take photographs. Sometimes people buy these works of art because they worry there will be no forests in the future, and they want a reminder of what the magnificent trees were once like.

The "Hollow Tree," Stanley Park, Vancouver, British Columbia. Even in 1928, people thought large trees were unusual. This redcedar stump is still standing. In the picture are the author's grandfather (at the rear) and the author's uncle (sitting in the car). Both worked as loggers.

CAMP WITH CARE

- Avoid damaging the soil and plants around your campsite.
- Use modern mattresses instead of branches for bedding.
- Use gas stoves if possible. If a fire is necessary, use only dead branches — don't cut down snags.
- Know how to prevent forest fires.
- Don't feed or disturb wildlife. Remember, you're in their home.

The natives took two to three days to cut down a tree by chipping and/or burning around the base. Fallen trunks were saved whole for canoes and totem poles, split into thick planks for houses, or cut for small carvings.

Without cedar, the Haida couldn't have created their civilization. Cedar is soft and easily carved. It's light, so big pieces can be moved by teams of men. It splits easily into long, straight, even

Before Europeans came to the Pacific Northwest, the Haida on B.C.'s Queen Charlotte Islands and Alaska's southern panhandle were the best canoe-makers on the coast. The Haida (their name means "the people") had no saws, nails or glue, and few metal tools, but they were able to build dugouts that carried them as far away as Puget Sound in present-day Washington State. Their biggest boats held three dozen people along with all their supplies.

Haida canoes were dug out of trunks of western redcedars. Each winter, Haida men went into the forest to cut tall straight cedars. They looked for trees with few branches or knots. They tested each tree for rot by thumping on the trunk to hear if it sounded hollow. If it seemed solid, they cut a hole into the center of the tree to make sure before chopping it down. You can still find trees with holes in them on the Charlottes, left standing because they weren't suitable.

boards. When steamed, it bends without splintering. Cedar looks good — it even smells good! The red wood contains a fragrant oil that repels insects and slows decay. Cedar houses and totems can still be seen in villages abandoned one hundred years ago.

Near such villages you can find living cedars that had their bark stripped long ago. Haida women collected cedar bark to weave into clothing and cover-

ings. Women also coiled the soft bark into rope, fish nets, baskets, and dozens of household items.

The rainforest provided many other useful plants. The Haida dug roots of Sitka spruce for weaving waterproof hats, picked salmonberries for food, and gathered peat moss for stuffing material. Wild plants provided medicine, dyes, and paint.

Today, some natives still gather plants in the forests that surround their villages. They eat wild food because it tastes good, they make traditional clothing to wear at cultural events, and they carve masks and other art to earn a living. They still need the western redcedar. The lifestyle of these people still depends on rainforest.

Millions of North Americans appreciate the outdoors. They like to camp and canoe and hike and fish and watch birds and take pictures, to name a few activities. The most superb places to do these things are national, state, and provincial parks along the coast — places where rainforest cutting is prohibited. As rainforests disappear, the remaining uncut valleys and parks are becoming more and more valuable.

Suddenly, people are realizing some of the world's most remarkable plants grow right in our own country. Some thought such giant trees were all gone. Others didn't even know North America had rainforests. They're now coming to see what they're losing, and to enjoy it before it's gone. So rainforest has another use to people — tourism. Gradually, people are beginning to understand trees are important for more than wood and paper.

Tourism is a growing industry in the Pacific Northwest. Adventure travel—trips that take visitors to see wildlife and wilderness—is very popular. No one spends their holiday in logged areas.

We also know rainforests are essential for the survival of fish and wildlife. Scientists tell us we need plants from temperate rainforests to search for new medicines (two have been found already). Foresters need to continue studying rainforest ecology to understand the role it plays in the health of the world. Too much depends on the rainforest to cut most of it down.

Canada and the United States have been cutting their ancient forests as if they would last forever. Logging, lumbering, pulp and paper have become big business in the west. Thousands of families, even whole towns, rely on trees to earn a living. That's because those who work in forest industries spend money at businesses that have no connection with the forest. In some mill towns, each forest employee supports about two other jobs. For example, the newspaper editor and the school teacher are able to work only because other families work in the woods and the mills and need their services.

The companies that employ forest workers don't want to lose money, otherwise they go out of business. So they cut more and more trees every year. Right now, over 400 square kilometers (154 square miles) of rainforest are cut in British Columbia each year — more than ever before, and faster than it can be replaced. Even the provincial Minister of Forests has admitted there will be a shortage of sawlogs in the future.

This means that in two or three decades, most of the virgin forests that can be cut for lumber will be gone. Replacement trees have been planted, but they won't be large enough to keep the mills working at the same rate. Then the forestry industry won't need as many people. Loggers and lumber workers are worried and angry about this because they will lose jobs.

Natives last lived in the abandoned Haida village of Ninstints in 1885, after occupying the site for 1,500 years. Although their houses have collapsed, two dozen totems still stand. Weathered and gray, the wood still shows carved animal and human figures. Hundreds of visitors come from all over the world to see these poles and marvel about this creative civilization.

In order to keep people employed, and to pay their bills, the forest companies would like to keep cutting rainforest until the replacement forests can be cut. In time, that will clear most ancient coastal forests as we know them. The Marbled Murrelet may be gone. Additional birds and animals may be on the endangered species list.

Right now, loggers feel resentful of other people telling them how to do their jobs. At the same time, British Columbia natives are upset that loggers often come to cut forests the natives believe they rightfully own. In recent years, tempers have become short as people of different viewpoints tried to force their wishes onto others.

You can't blame forest workers for worrying about their jobs. Today, another threat to worker livelihood has appeared. Use of machines in the logging and lumbering business has reduced the number of jobs by half over the past 30 years. Because the machines make the work easier and faster, fewer people are needed to cut the same number of trees. Workers have been steadily losing jobs all along, just because of technology.

But if we continue as we have, other people who depend on the forest will be affected as well. The salmon will lose their homes, so commercial fishermen will be out of work. Outdoor guides will lose business because nobody wants to visit areas without trees or wildlife.

Life for everyone on earth is changing because we didn't believe we would ever run out of resources. With so few rainforests left (in temperate zones as well as the tropics), people are thinking hard about the future of all environments. They want governments to save more land as parks, where the natural environment cannot be disturbed.

In British Columbia, just over six percent of the province is saved as parks. Costa Rica, a small country in Central America, has nine percent of its land in national parks, and nearly all of these parks contain tropical rainforest. The B.C. government saves less of its own territory than poorer countries that have a greater need for cleared land. The United Nations has recommended that countries set aside twelve percent of their land for parks.

Additional parks would help preserve temperate rainforest. So why not make more parks now? More visitors would come to see the rainforest and enjoy nature. Tourists would be good for business, without ruining our environment.

Some people already know this. In recent years, whale-watching tours have become very popular on the west coast. Former logging communities are becoming known internationally for salmon fishing, rainforest trails, or as places where artists find inspiration. All along the coast, you can find yacht charters, lodges, airplane companies, and other businesses that visitors need. These are encouraging trends, and show one way towns can keep citizens working by having more than one industry.

The logging industry could also do more with the wood that it cuts. Oregon, for example, sends whole and split logs to the Orient, where someone else cuts them into lumber. And British Columbia ships nearly all of its wood out of the country, where other sawmills cut the rough lumber into smaller pieces for things such as furniture, doors, windows, railings, and moldings.

All this means less work for the logging communities themselves. This upsets unemployed forest workers who need work to care for their children. It's a practice they want stopped.

Comparing B.C. to other places with large forest industries, we find Sweden with two-and-a-half times the number of jobs for the same amount of wood cut. The United States creates about three times as many jobs. Both these countries use B.C. lumber. That means Canadians are doing themselves a poor turn. If we're really worried that cutting fewer trees means fewer jobs, we should be operating more mills that make wood products, to create alternative jobs for loggers.

Some new jobs have already been created in B.C. The government has helped to start businesses by buying seedlings from nurseries, by employing contractors to plant and prune young trees, and by hiring special machinery to treat soil and create better growing sites. As forests become more intensively researched and managed in the future, other types of work will be available for workers.

Slowly, the science of forestry is evolving. It's evident our reliance on clear-cutting as the primary way to log must end. There *are* other ways, including

LET TREES BE GREEN, NOT GARBAGE

It takes one tree three times taller than a telephone pole to provide the wood and paper products used each year by the average North American. Most of our garbage is paper and wood, so every time you throw away a paper bag, a cardboard box, or scrap lumber, you cause more trees to be cut down. Here are some ways to reduce, reuse, and recycle wood products:

- Use scrap pieces of lumber for hobby projects or for firewood.
- Buy writing paper and toilet paper made from recycled paper.
- Write on both sides of pages. Make notepaper out of scrap paper.
- Use cloth handkerchiefs, towels, and napkins instead of throw-away tissues, paper towels, and paper napkins.
- Recycle newspapers at home, and writing and computer paper at school. Each tonne (2,240 pounds) of recycled paper produced saves 17 trees and 31,000 liters (8,180 gallons) of clean water.
- Give old magazines to a friend, to a used book store, or to a hospital.
- Drink from reusable or recyclable glass bottles instead of paper containers and cups.
- Take your own shopping bag to the supermarket.
- Carry your lunch in a lunch box instead of a paper bag.
- If your school cafeteria uses paper plates, ask them to use real dishes — or take your own.
- Don't buy things that have unnecessary paper packaging. Tell the store manager and write to the company and tell them why you do this.
- Do your parents use disposable diapers on your brother or sister? Ask them to consider cloth diapers instead.

Conifer seedlings in a
forest nursery.

logging only some trees at a time. One method developed in recent years in Washington and Oregon is called "New Forestry." It is designed to create a forest of mixed tree size, age, and type. Among other things, New Forestry calls for

- managing forests as broad landscapes, not as fragmented cut-blocks;
- logging that leaves standing green trees and snags;
- leaving logs and debris on the ground to rot and enrich the soil;
- leaving wide unlogged corridors along streams and rivers;
- planting mixed replacement species, including deciduous (broad-leaved) trees;
- cutting forests less often, so they have a chance to mature;
- protecting soil from damage by machines and erosion.

New Forestry will help the trees, fish, wildlife and humans. But it has disadvantages as well. The wood products we use every day will become more expensive. Less wood will be cut. There could be increased danger to forest workers.

Forest companies are not fully convinced New Forestry will benefit them, but they have begun to experiment with it.

Clear-cutting might still be used occasionally in the future, but companies must try this new forestry wherever possible. There is much to learn as forest management moves into a new era. Forest planning must involve people with different ideas — ideas that consider the environment as well as economics. And before we cut much more, a plan is necessary to preserve and maintain ancient coastal forests for ecological excellence, not just as renewable resources.

WHAT CAN YOU DO?

- Write to business and government leaders or your local newspaper about what you would like done about the rainforest. Ask the government how it is planning for a different economy.

- Raise money for rainforest, wildlife, or salmon conservation projects. Donate the money to an organization that tells you what they do with it, or volunteer to work yourself.

- Join a group that studies or protects parks and forest areas. Ask them for information on what they do and how you can help.

- Ask your teacher to bring in a park naturalist, a nature tour operator, a professional forester, or forest industry employee to tell you more about rainforests. Ask them to show pictures of their work.

- Ask your principal to match your school with a coastal school, and exchange rainforest projects with students in classes similar to your own. Maybe it would be possible to visit your student "twins."

- Visit a lumber or pulp mill, tree nursery, national or state park, or experimental forest with your family or class. Learn all you can about who manages the forest and what they use it for.

Temperate rainforests of the Pacific Northwest are among the special places on the planet. Time and the forest are running out. If we are to stop this, we must make choices. Each choice is difficult, and each has consequences. You have a right to your say.

What would you like to do about the last of the green giants?

Index